RIGHT ENDPAPER

EDWARD GOREY

·A·M·P·H·I·G·O·R·E·Y·

·A·L·S·O·

CONGDON & WEED, INC., NEW YORK

Copyright © 1983 by Edward Gorey
Library of Congress Catalog Card Number: 83-71334
ISBN 0-86553-087-4
ISBN 0-312-92023-7 (St. Martin's Press)
Published by Congdon & Weed, Inc.
298 Fifth Avenue, New York, N.Y. 10001
Distributed by St. Martin's Press
175 Fifth Avenue, New York, N.Y. 10010
Published simultaneously in Canada by
Methuen Publications
2330 Midland Avenue, Agincourt, Ontario M1S 1P7
Printed in the United States of America
First Edition

For the dog at Gay Head, 27.iv.83

CONTENTS

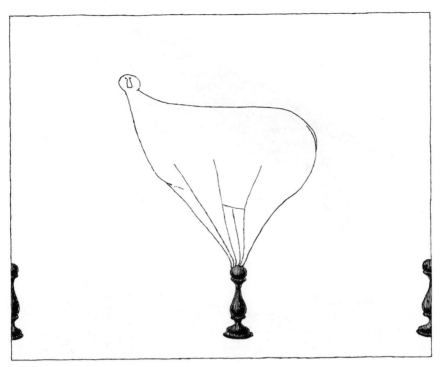

The Ampoo is intensely neat;
Its head is small, likewise its feet.

The Boggerslosh conceals itself
In back of bottles on a shelf.

The Crunk is not unseldom drastic
And must be hindered by elastic.

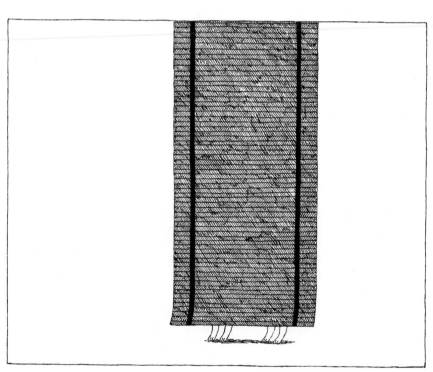

The Dawbis is remote and shy;
It shuns the gaze of passers-by.

The Epitwee's inclined to fits
Until at last it falls to bits.

The Fidknop is devoid of feeling;
It drifts about beneath the ceiling.

The Gawdge is understood to save
All sorts of objects in its cave.

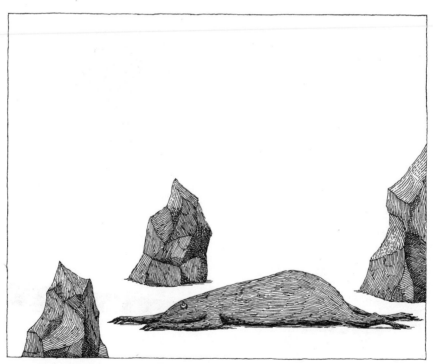

The Humglum crawls along the ground,
And never makes the slightest sound.

The Ippagoggy has a taste
For every kind of glue and paste.

The Jelbislup cannot get far
Because it's kept inside a jar.

The Kwongdzu has enormous claws;
Its character is full of flaws.

The Limpflig finds it hard to keep
From spending all its life asleep.

The Mork proceeds with pensive grace
And no expression on its face.

The Neapse's sufferings are chronic;
It lives exclusively on tonic.

The Ombledroom is vast and white,
And therefore visible by night.

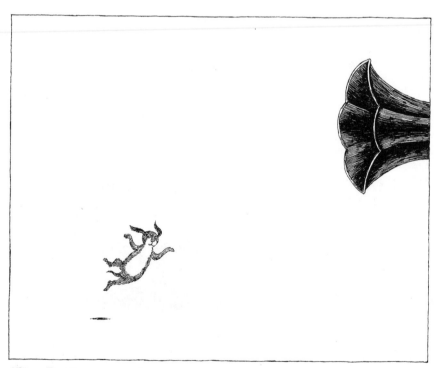

The Posby goes into a trance
In which it does a little dance.

The Quingawaga squeaks and moans
While dining off of ankle bones.

The Raitch hangs downward from its tail
By knotting it around a nail.

The Scrug's extremely nasty-looking,
And is unusable for cooking.

The Twibbit on occasion knows
A difficulty with its toes.

The Ulp is very, very small;
It hardly can be seen at all.

The Veazy makes a creaking noise;
It has no dignity or poise.

The Wambulus has floppy ears
With which to wipe away its tears.

The Xyke stands up at close of day,
And then it slowly walks away.

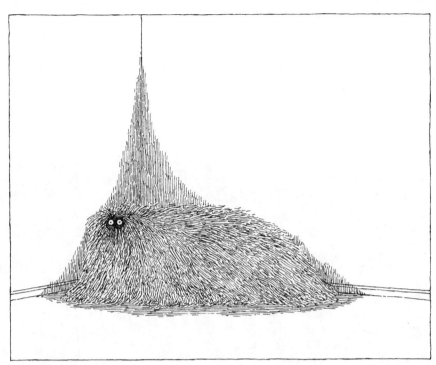

The Yawfle stares, and stares, and stares,
And stares, and stares, and stares, and stares.

About the Zote what can be said?
There was just one, and now it's dead.

DER
TRAURIGE
ZWÖLFPFÜNDER.

EDWARD GOREY: THE BLUE ASPIC

Jasper Ankle stood all night in a drizzle to buy a third-gallery ticket for *La vengeance posthume*.

While dressing, Gertrúdis Callosidad dipped into a box of candied violets from an unknown admirer.

Ortenzia Caviglia, hitherto unheard, went on instead; her
'Vide le cerceuil, vide mon coeur' put the audience into raptures.

After the performance she was invited to supper by the head
of the opera, Baron von Knöchel.

Jasper sat up until dawn by himself.

By the end of the season Caviglia had sung *Gli occhielli*, *Lizzia Bordena*, *La reine des iguanes*, *Julietta di Lavenza*, and was talked about everywhere.

Instead of writing labels, Jasper read and reread the clippings about Caviglia hidden in his desk.

Ortenzia's manager, Ambrogio Rigaglie, fell down the elevator shaft at a costumer's, but Herakleitos Vithilogos took his place.

Jasper went without lunch three days running to buy Caviglia's recording of 'Vivi con una mira' from *Il fiore sotto il piede*.

Caviglia appeared in a series of advertisements for Grudge's Cucumber Soap.

Jasper stood all night in a freezing rain to buy a third-gallery ticket for *Die Chinesische Brille*.

As Tsi-Nan-Fu Caviglia had her greatest triumph to date.

Jasper got pneumonia, and was dismissed from his job.

The famous Spoffish emeralds were given to Caviglia by the Duke of Whaup.

Without his clippings, Jasper now wrote long letters to Ortenzia, which went unanswered.

Agnes Alice Popover, Ortenzia's nearest rival, was discovered strangled with a scarf she wore in *Teodora*.

Jasper's gramophone got smashed as he was being evicted from his rooms.

Caviglia was painted by Sergissopov as Mae in *The Dubious Errand*.

Jasper wandered the streets, his warping records clutched to his chest.

A statue fell on the Duke of Whaup during the second interval of *Amable Tastu*.

Jasper was apprehended in the wings as Caviglia sang 'Una tazza di cacao' at a rehearsal of *L'avvelenatrice di Glasgovia*.

Caviglia's revival of *Elagabalo* was cut short when the authorities had the curtain rung down on the triple-wedding scene.

Jasper was committed to an asylum where no gramophone was available to the inmates.

Caviglia cruised the Adriatic with Basil Zaribaydjian, the financier, on his yacht, the *Maud*.

Jasper's records got broken as he was escaping from the asylum.

M. Gazogène, the leader of Mme Pince-Oreille's claque, impaled himself on a skewer affixed to his seat during *Gomiti di rammarico*.

Jasper stood all night in a blizzard to buy a third-gallery ticket for the premiere of *Nera Agnese di Dunbar*.

Ortenzia had a premonition while holding the A above high C at the climax of 'Ah, paese dei bovini hispidi!'.

As she left the opera house with the Maharajah of Eschnapur, Jasper rose up from behind a snowdrift and stabbed her in the throat.

He then stabbed himself and crying 'J'ai trouvé Hortense!', fell dead on her corpse.

PROLOGUE

It was the day after Tuesday and the day before Wednesday.

CHAPTER ONE

Embley and Yewbert were hitting one another with croquet mallets

when they heard a noise behind the wall

and an untenanted bicycle rolled into view.

CHAPTER TWO

Brother and sister tried to take sole possession of it

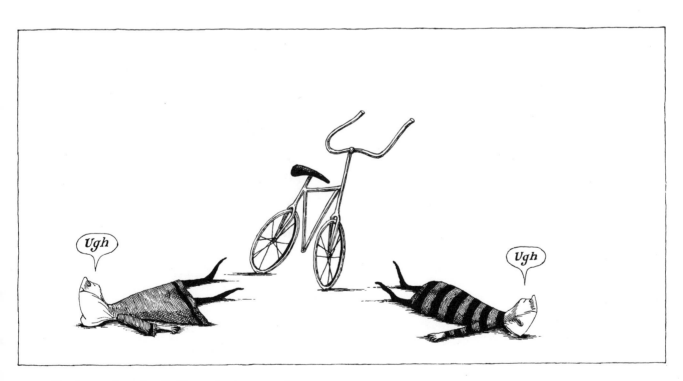

until they both fell exhausted;

Yewbert recovered first and leapt onto the seat

so Embley had to sit on the handlebars as they flew out the gate.

CHAPTER FOUR

After that they almost ran into a tree

on which was perched a large bird

who muttered as they went by.

CHAPTER SEVEN

They rode past a great many turnip fields

but as it was the wrong time of year, they didn't see any turnips.

CHAPTER ELEVEN

A horrid storm came up;

they were nearly *struck* **by** lightning

several times.

When it was over Embley found she had lost her fourteen pairs of yellow shoes

and Yewbert his spotted-fur waistcoat.

CHAPTER TWELVE

As they were riding through a lengthy puddle

an alligator rose up in front of them;

Embley kicked it on the end of its nose, and it expired.

CHAPTER FIFTEEN

They took a wrong turning and before they knew it, were entering a vast barn;

it was too dark to hear anything;

it fell down as they came out the other end.

CHAPTER NINETEEN

They made for a huge bush

off which they rapidly ate a quantity of berries.

They returned home

to discover there was nothing to be seen but an obelisk

which said it had been raised to their memory 173 years ago;

the bicycle uttered for the last time and fell to bits.

The Sopping Thursday by Edward Gorey

It must be somewhere

Since early morning it has been raining

Where is my umbrella?

I do not like carrying an umbrella

The cats are nervous when it is raining

The child has somehow got shut inside its umbrella

Nor do I really care for this umbrella.

The infant is saved from being swept down the open sewer because the dog has recognized its master's umbrella

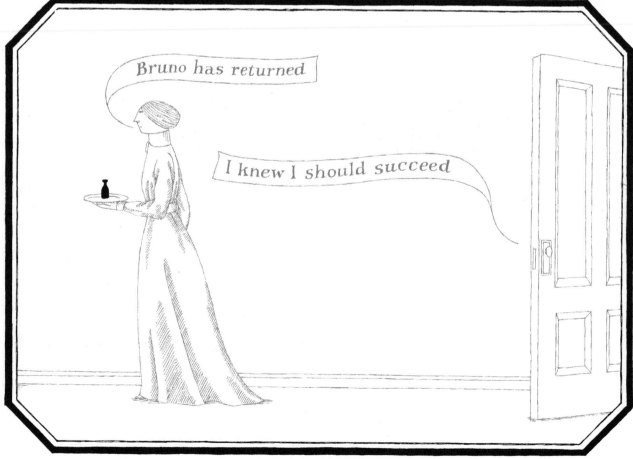

Bruno has returned

I knew I should succeed

THE GRAND PASSION

A NOVEL

Englished anonymously
from the Conton Dialect (1930)
and illustrated by
EDWARD GOREY

What trees is this?

You are not able to catch me.

This flower has opened very beautifully.

I have lost one thing.

Where is your dress?

How did you break this plate?

This room is too narrow.

It is always in the same way.

That *is* the bad of all.

What kind of disease have you?

There has just descended one shower of rain.

That place leaks dreadfully.

I tell you the truth it is not so.

That is altogether different from this.

When are you going to embrak?

The Eclectic Abecedarium

Betray no qualms
When asked for Alms.

A hidden Bird
Is often heard.

Pick up loose Crumbs
Upon your thumbs.

Look back before
You close a Door.

There is an Eye
Up in the sky.

It takes elan
To wield a Fan.

Beyond the Glass
We see life pass.

For catching Hail
Keep by a pail.

Be loath to drink
Indian Ink.

Don't try to cram
The dog with Jam.

In sorting Kelp
Be quick to help.

Forbear to taste
Library Paste.

Be sure a Mouse
Lurks in the house.

A careless No
Leads on to woe.

Don't leave the shore
Without an Oar.

Request a Pill
When you are ill.

Find tasks to do
While in a Queue.

Attempt to cope
With tangled Rope.

See down the Sun
When day is done.

On any road
May sit a Toad.

Don't overturn
The garden Urn.

Beware the Vine
Which can entwine.

The way to Hell
Is down a Well.

The letter X
Was made to vex.

With every Yawn
A moment's gone.

The kitchen sink
Is made of Zinc.

It is not the living, it is the being lived on.

I must remember to write that, along with some other things, down.

One day a week I don't _____, but I never tell anyone which day it is.

Last week it was Thursday, wasn't it?

It seems to me wine warms up very quickly.

I never know what you think is important.

The _____s have it all over us.

Only if you live there.

I never insult you in front of others.

I keep forgetting that everything you say is connected.

I should like a parsley sandwich.

To the best of my knowledge they are not in season.

Not everything in life can be interpreted metaphorically.

That's because things fall out on the way.

As I always say.

I know you do, although I don't believe I've ever actually heard you.

Kampan'yō-isu no ryōkin wa tokubetsu ni ikura desu ka?

Kibun ga warui.

What is the extra charge for a deck chair?

I feel sick.

It seems to me a fate worse than sinking.

But there isn't any other kind.

I understand _____ *is an author.*

I am not certain I can arrange an introduction.

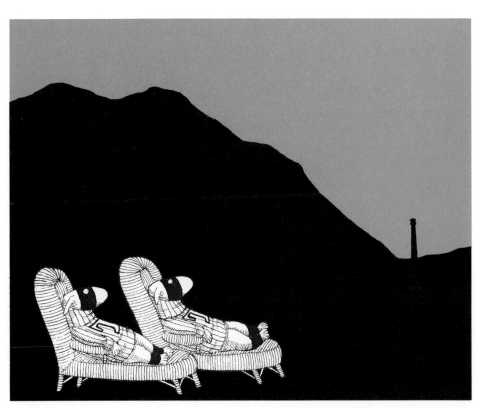

More is happening out there than we are aware of.

It is possibly due to some unknown direful circumstance.

I thought it was going to be different;
It turned out to be(,) just the same.

What is Food?
It's a small town in New Hampshire.

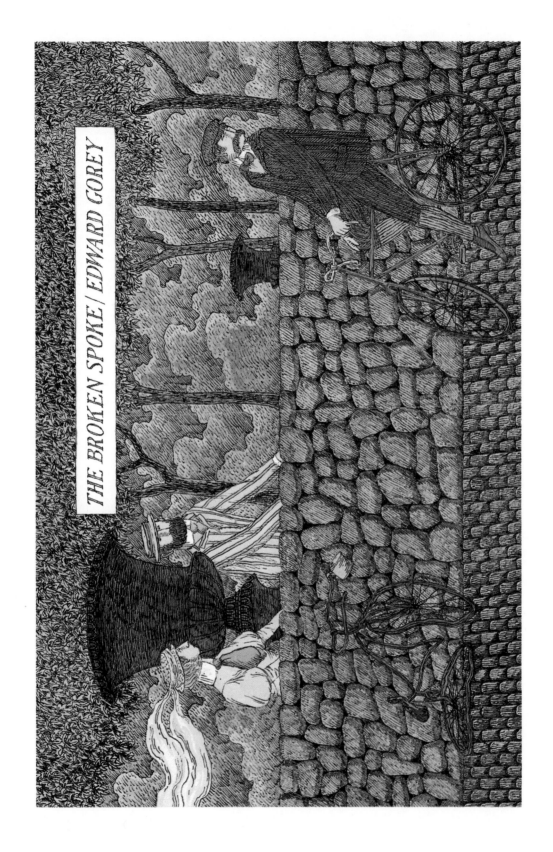

THE BROKEN SPOKE / EDWARD GOREY

CYCLING CARDS

FROM THE **PEN** *of* DOGEAR WRYDE

The First Ride

Monsieur Bandage-Herniaire and his famous Unreflecting Bicycle

Contestants in the annual Trans-Novaya Zemlya Bicycle Race

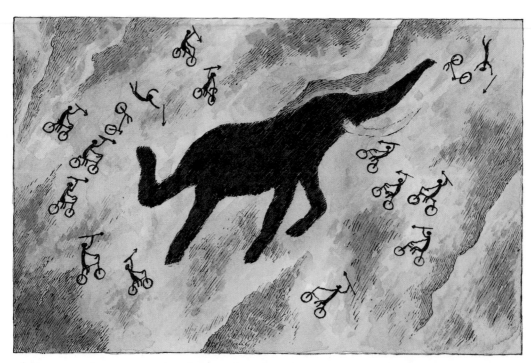

After a photograph of a painting found on the wall of a cave near Afazia, Ohio, the location of the entrance to which is no longer known

The Crumbath Cyclery by moonlight

DAFFODIL
*who, according
to her owner,
Col H. Proon,
has in less than
twelve years
bitten over
17,000 cyclists
in the ankle*

Laurel Villa

Bicycle worship in the Tediola Archipelago

*The Martyrdom of St Egfroth. Eleventh century drawing,
Hollowtooth Museum, Mortshire*

Miss A. Sprigknot, the first lady to cross the suspension bridge over Porphyria Falls on a bicycle

The Cycle Cemetery near Dingy Cruet, Blots

Major O'Twiddy, the hero of Falling Forks. Anonymous water-colour, c.1825

Celebrated Cycling Calamities No. 23. The Duke of Aught suffers a puncture on his way to the first performance of Crudele, Queen of Corinth in 178 years

The rescue of Sir Odo Fitzaddle from the top of Mt Radish

The Broken Spoke

Innocence, on the Bicycle of Propriety, carrying the Urn of Reputation safely over the Abyss of Indiscretion

The Crumpet-Fanlight Expedition : Capt. Mousegrave's fatal reconnaissance at Ulna Bay

The Orange Bicycle Case: the discovery of Nesba Macsplosh's head

Ex-voto, formerly in the possession of G. E. Deadworry

Exploits of the Bicycle Bandit: the seizure of the Marchioness of Bunworry's emeralds during a ball at Condiment House

Arthur Igleby, the long-distance champion, working out on Nattering Sands

Nineteenth century Japanese stencil: bats and bicycles

Apparition of demon cyclist that appeared in the sky over Gasket, Maine several times during the second week in November, 1911

THE PEDALLING PALLUDINIS

Valse dégueulasse

THE POSTCARD MYSTERY

BY D. AWDREY-GORE

The Blancmange Tragedy

D. Awdrey-Gore

The Toastrack Enigma

D. Awdrey-Gore

THE AWDREY-GORE LEGACY

EDWARD GOREY

They dazzle us, but can we trust
These pictures drawn upon the dust?

THE IPSIAD, *can.V*

INTRODUCTORY NOTE BY E. G. DEADWORRY

On last St Spasmus's day Miss D. Awdrey-Gore was found dead at the age of 97. Just before dawn a nameless poacher came upon her body in a disused fountain on the estate of Lord Ravelflap; she was seated bolt upright on a gilt ballroom chair, one of a set of seventeen then on display at Suthick & Upter's Auction Rooms in Market Footling; her left hand clutched a painted tin lily of cottage manufacture, inside which was rolled up a Cad's Relish label of a design superseded in 1947; something illegible was pencilled on the back. That she had been murdered was obvious, though as yet the cause of death has not been determined.

One moment she was sitting there;
The next, she'd vanished into air.

THE IPSIAD, *can.VI*

It will be remembered that Miss Awdrey-Gore
was one of the most prolific (*vide* our Two-Shilling
Reprint Library) and celebrated writers of
detective stories at the time of her unexpected
disappearance on St Spasmus's eve in 1927. On
various occasions since then, she has been
reported (among a number of other possibilities)
in a private lunatic asylum, living in Taormina
dressed as a man, married to a Salubrian nobleman
in Slobgut, or alternately, a garage mechanic in
Idle-on-Sea, in religious retreat on the slopes of
Kanchenjunga. But always falsely: her whereabouts
for the past forty-four years remain unknown.

Several days after her reappearance, in a nearby suburban villa an oiled-silk packet came to light beneath the false bottom of an elephant's foot umbrella stand. Done up with mauve string and indigo blue sealing wax, it was addressed to my late grand-father, G. E. Deadworry, then (in 1927) head of Deadworry and Silt, her publishers. The packet's contents in their entirety—though certain things are patently missing—are reproduced on the following pages.

Waredo Dyrge
Half Irish, half Japanese
Has been soldier of fortune and progressive
    victim of explosions all over the world
Now England's most sought-after private
    detective
Has possibly world's most valuable collection
    of artificial hands, many of them given to
    him by grateful clients
Will never take up a case on a Tuesday

To catch and keep the public's gaze
One must have lots of little ways.
                        THE IPSIAD, can.IV

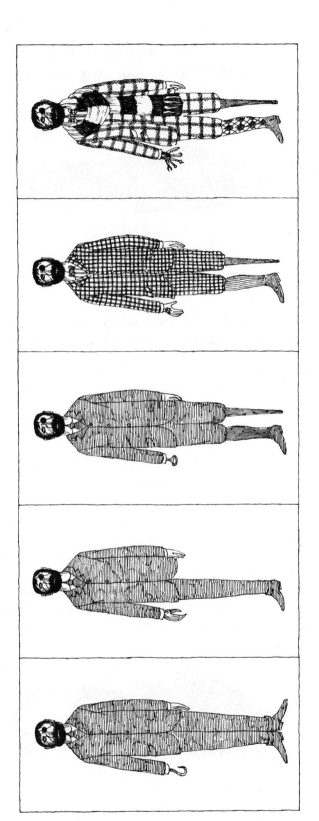

His deductions concerning each case are given in the form of a linked series of haiku in Gaelic of his own composition; each is presented to the reader as it is made in a literal English translation that, while strange and vague in the extreme, turns out to have been perfectly fair and even obvious.

Deary, his inseparable and ferocious companion, is named for his master's favourite reading – the Deary Rewdgo Series for Intrepid Young Ladies (D.R. on the Great Divide, D.R. in the Yukon, D.R. at Baffin Bay, etc.) by Dewda Yorger. He is familiar with thirty-seven different hand signals, and has a passionate fondness for Cad's Relish on water biscuits.

Owner of great estate   Local magistrate
Baronet   M.F.H.   Member of Parliament

Of all the people on the scene
Some are betwixt and some
between.

THE IPSIAD, can. II

County/not quite county lady   Owner of fabulous
jewels   Hostess of weekend house party

Heroine (if she turns out to be the murderer,
have a second with different hair colour)

Curate/Vicar/Dean/Bishop   Escaped lunatic
Cousin from Tasmania

Amateur cricketer/sailor/explorer   Architect
Heir to title and/or estate   Childhood friend

Duke/Dowager duchess   Village ancient   Superannuated governess/gardener

Member of the upper class gone to the bad   Lower class person with a grudge

Lady novelist   Lady with passion for Flowers/dogs/other ladies   Scottish cousin

Author of standard work on string figures   Indigent cousin   Axe murderess in forgotten *cause célèbre*

Unsuccessful poet   Successful interior decorator   Unsuitable friend of heroine/hero

Real/bogus Middle European nobleman   Gigolo   Secret agent for us them

Doctor Solicitor Secretary Friend of family Spy
Jewel thief Cousin who inherits everything

Postmistress Housekeeper Seamstress
Companion Cousin who is retired missionary

Provincial music-hall star Owner of fashionable
supper club Nurse Cousin by marriage

American millionaire Newspaper proprietor
Prime minister Condiment tycoon

The authorities : local / Scotland Yard

Famous/notorious actress Unsuitable friend of
hero/heroine Cousin living at Antibes

Shell grotto

It's most unlikely that his bed
Is where the victim's lying dead.
THE IPSIAD, *Can.III*

Ha-ha

Standing stone

Library

Dinghy

Empty tenement

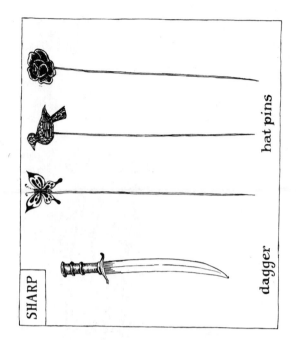

SHARP

dagger   hat pins

He was, it's said, somehow done in
With nothing but a safety pin.
THE IPSIAD, can. VI

POISONOUS

face powder   blowgun darts   hors d'oeuvres

aperitif   library paste

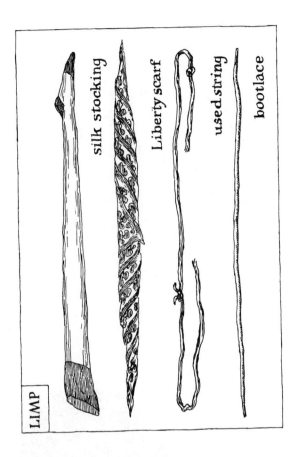

LIMP

silk stocking

Liberty scarf

used string

bootlace

BLUNT

lead spoon

marble baluster

stone idol

INEXPLICABLE

confetti

GRADUAL

arsenical buns

INSTANTANEOUS

boulder

INFERNAL MACHINES

eight feet, seven inches

papier-mâché animal

tea cosy

telephone doll

match box

darning egg

scented soap

wax pear

To West Prune
Tower
Factory
Reservoir
To East Prune
Cottage
To South Prune

The crucial information can
Be hidden in a simple plan.
THE IPSIAD, can. VIII

Cross section of fountain from west showing faulty pipe

The labyrinth at 4:09 when Harold Tyne-Forque gave up trying to reach its heart

The labyrinth at 3:27 after Miss Gentian had **successfully** found her way in and back

The Celery Room
Showing position of vases and rug

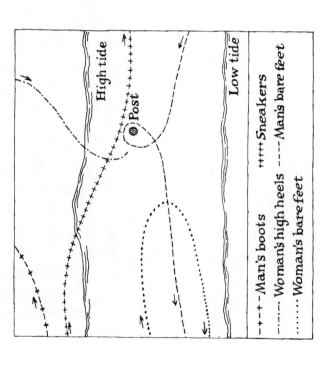

High tide

Post

Low tide

+-+-+- Man's boots ++++ Sneakers ----- Man's bare feet

------- Woman's high heels

.... Woman's bare feet

The smallest clue may be (or not)
The one to give away the plot.
THE IPSIAD, *can. I*

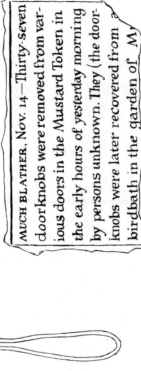

MUCH BLATHER, Nov. 14 — Thirty-seven doorknobs were removed from various doors in the Mustard Token in the early hours of yesterday morning by persons unknown. They (the doorknobs were later recovered from a birdbath in the garden of M

,,

Nº 704G

On the 14th of January, the 'Larko Sandange' was still off the coast of Iceland

---

What the murderer failed to realize is that Grumbletch's salts are not soluble in lemonade

---

_____ is _____ Lady Truss _____ really two entirely different people

---

What the murderer failed to realize is that at high tide the outcrop of Saint Leolai's Rocks is completly submerged

---

At 11:17 the door to the winter garden _____ was already locked and bolted

---

James Grumesdaul and _____ Charles Trast _____ are really the same person

---

What the murderer failed to realize is that the Great Northwest Road does not go beyond Little Remorse

---

George Utmost _____ is really not Daphne Loot _____'s cousin from Wyoming

---

Perhaps it might be even subtler
If after all it *was* the butler.
THE IPSIAD, *can. IX*

What the murderer failed to realize is that there is no Number Fourteen, Bandage Terrace

---

Lola Trope _____ is really _____ Lord Onion _____'s great-grand-daughter

---

What the murderer failed to realize is that yellow stitchbane is not yellow at all, but a pale mauve

Hanging

The guilty found, there's little wait
Before they're overcome by fate.
THE IPSIAD, *can. xiii*

Cyanide pill

Over the cliff

Madness

Successful escape

Unsuccessful escape

The Great ▬ern Road

And what if then we don't find out
What all of it has been about?

THE IPSIAD, *can. XI*

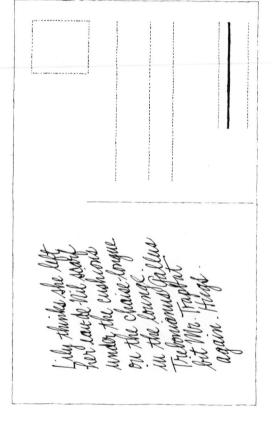

Lily thinks she left
her eau-de-nil scarf
under the cushions
on the chaise-longue
in the lounge
Trebonianusgallus
but Mrs. Traplet
again. Hegi

No. 1)   Terrace,   Chester

These postcards recently fell out of a discarded lending-library copy of *The Teacosy Crime*, perhaps Miss Awdrey-Gore's most popular work. It will be noticed they were never sent, or, for that matter, even addressed.

Post card Carte postale Postkarte Cartolina postale
Dopisnice Открытое письмо Levelezö-Lap Briefkaart.

*Send at once
recipe for
plaice with
thyme.*

THE ▮▮▮▮ ROCKS
OFF THE ▮▮▮▮SHIRE COAST,
▮▮▮▮ LIGHT
IN DISTANCE

Post Card

I did it.
E. G. Deadworthy

The creature regarded them Balefully.

She wandered among the trees Aimlessly.

The pudding was served Clumsily.

They played whist Distractedly.

She knitted mufflers Endlessly.

They searched the cellars Fruitlessly.

She danced on the sands Giddily.

He looked out the window Hopelessly.

He fell off the pier Inadvertently.

She toyed with her beads Jadedly.

They got themselves up Killingly.

He exposed himself Lewdly.

He ran through the hall Maniacally.

He *sat* in the train Numbly.

The doorbell rang Ominously.

It was in the trunk Presumably.

She let go of it Quickly.

He spoke to the child Repressively.

He disposed of the fragments Slyly.

She ran out of the room Tearfully.

He explained himself Unconvincingly.

She appeared on the roof Vapourously.

He struck her down Wilfully.

The piece was sung eXcruciatingly.

She watched him go Yearningly.

He wrote it all down Zealously.

THE

LOATHSOME COUPLE

EDWARD GOREY

Harold Snedleigh was found beating a sick small animal
to death with a rock, when he was five years old.

That year Mona Gritch was born to a pair of drunkards.

By the time he was twelve Harold had caught the cold that
afterwards never left him.

As a child Mona already had thick ankles and thin hair.

After leaving school Harold went to work in a plumber's office, and stole curiosa from booksellers whenever he got the chance.

Mona was employed behind the jewelry counter in a five-and-ten, amusing herself by loosening settings with a nailfile so the stones would fall out soon after purchase.

The two met at a Self-Help Institute lecture on the Evils of
the Decimal System, and immediately recognized their affinity.

On Sundays they took long walks together, and Harold
would bring one of his books.

They went to the local cinema whenever there was a crime
film playing.

Following one particularly exciting one, they fumbled with each other in a cold woodshed.

After several years they secretly rented a remote and
undesirable villa.

When they tried to make love, their strenuous and
prolonged efforts came to nothing.

In the autumn of that year they decided to embark upon
their life's work.

Months later, after many complicated preparations, they
felt at last they were ready.

Mona lured a little girl named Eepie Carpetrod to the villa with promises of a doll wearing a green satin frock.

They spent the better part of the night murdering the
child in various ways.

By twilight of the next day the body was buried and
the mess cleaned up.

They sat down to a meal of cornflakes and treacle, turnip sandwiches, and artificial grape soda.

The pictures Mona had taken did not come out very well,
being underexposed, but they put them in the new album
they had bought anyway.

Over the next two years they killed three more children,
but it was never as exhilarating as the first one had been.

For no very good reason their activities remained unsuspected.

Then one day in April some snapshots fell out of Harold's pocket on a tram.

At times they said they had done it all, but other times
they denied everything.

Someone threw a putrescent rat in Mona's face as she was being taken into the building where the court was.

The trial went on and on with both of them sunk in apathy.

They were found guilty but insane.

They were taken to the asylum in the same van but after
that they never saw each other again.

When he was forty-three Harold's cold turned into pneumonia and he died within a few days.

Mona failed to such an extent that for most of her life she did nothing but lick spots on the walls.

She died at the age of eighty-two or eighty-four.

The mother of Little Tancred sent him into the twilight
to buy three pennies' worth of tapioca with which
to make their evening meal.

Before he had as yet not got even half-way he saw a
disturbed person whose sex was unclear coming
towards him while it waved its hands about.

Little Tancred started for the other side of the street, the three pennies falling from his grasp in the middle, but the Disturbed Person was there before him.

'Is this a visionary child I see, or are you really Tiny Clorinda?' cried the Disturbed Person, chewing on a string of green beads it wore around its neck.

'No—for my name is Little Tancred. If it is of my infant
sister you speak, good sir,' he ventured politely 'she
died last autumn from a disorder of the spine
brought on by a lack of nourishing food'.

'How it knocks my heart!' moaned the Disturbed Person,
its teeth rending the string asunder, the green beads
flying in all directions and vanishing into the grimy
drifts of snow.

'I am the Baroness von Rettig,' she announced 'your grandmother', and so Little Tancred led her back to where they lived.

In her astonishment at seeing her son in the company of a disturbed person on the doorstep, Little Tancred's mother forgot to ask the whereabouts of the tapioca.

When she was told who the Disturbed Person was, she explained 'We thought you were lost when the *Moon of Valparaiso* went down in the bay three years ago last April.

'Wilhelm, your only child,' she went on 'died of pneumonia contracted after helping to man the breeches-buoy all night in vain; those of us who are left visit the cemetery on the seventh of every month.

'But if you are not lying on the bottom of the sea,' she added 'can it be possible that your emerald necklace is not there after all either?'.

'Grandmother, when I met her,' put in Little Tancred 'was chewing some green beads, but they broke and rolled away'.

It was now quite dark both indoors and out and so a lantern was lit, and all three rushed into the street.

They hunted and hunted, but in the end found only one green bead, and that proved to be a glass marble belonging to a more fortunate little boy named Hugo who lived farther up the block.

One winter morning Friedrich woke
With an idea for a joke.

'I won't get up to-day;' he said
'I'll spend it lying here in bed'.

They came and called him through the door;
He only went to sleep once more.

They wondered if he'd fallen ill,
And asked if he would like a pill.

They offered, as a special treat,
To give him anything to eat.

That afternoon they brought new toys,
And other things for making noise.

They said he could do what he chose;
He only hid beneath the clothes.

As they gave up and left to stay,
The light was fading from the day.

'I'll get up now,' he thought 'and go
And play till supper in the snow'.

But when he tried to rise at last
The sheets and blankets held him fast.

A dreadful twang came from the springs;
The bed unfolded great black wings.

While Friedrich screamed, the bed took flight
And flapped away into the night.

They could not see it very soon
Because there wasn't any moon.

The bed came down again at dawn,
Both Friedrich and the bed-clothes gone.

THE TUNING FORK BY EDUARD BLUTIG

Eduard Blutig's Der Zeitirrthum
in a translation by Mrs Regera Dowdy
with the original pictures by O. Müde

Theoda was a homely child
Whose presence drove her family wild.

Her conversation and her dress
Alike inspired them with distress.

Theoda, bent on suicide,
Rushed down to meet the rising tide.

She cried 'Farewell!' to empty air,
And leapt off of the jetty there.

She sank; the water chilled her limbs;
She recollected bits of hymns.

She sank—until her senseless toes
Came into contact with a nose.

When she revived, she was not dead,
But on the ocean's floor instead.

A monster of alarming size
Was peering at her in surprise.

Despite this sudden change of fate,
She soon began to perorate.

The simple creature was aghast
At hearing of her cruel past.

Next day her joyful family found
Her father by the bathtub, drowned.

The same thing happened, one by one,
To all the rest. How was it done?

Theoda, having wanted curls,
Now draped her head with ropes of pearls.

The natives, afterwards, took fright
When she was seen, off shore, at night.